For Vicki
I hope *y*
Wishing *y*
Focusing. Susan

I never think
dark will come

Susan Jordan

Oversteps Books

First published in 2021 by   Oversteps Books Ltd
6 Halwell House
South Pool
Nr Kingsbridge
Devon
TQ7 2RX
UK

www.overstepsbooks.com

Printed in Great Britain by imprint digital, Devon

To all those beings, human and other-than-human,
who continue to teach me about life and poetry.

Acknowledgements

Poems in this collection have been published in the following online and print magazines: *The Broadsheet, The Dawntreader, The Drabble, The Fat Damsel, I am not a silent poet, Nutshells and Nuggets, Snakeskin* and *The Stare's Nest*, in the Paper Swans anthology *The Chronicles of Eve* and in the *Moor Poets anthology* Vol. IV.

My thanks to everyone who has given me support and helped me to compile this collection: Helen Evans, Jennie Osborne, Sue Proffitt and members of my Bath Spa alumnae writing group: Tanya Atapattu, Hadiza El-Rufai, Victoria Finlay, Emma Geen, Sophie McGovern, Jane Shemilt, Mimi Thebo and Vanessa Vaughan. My especial thanks to Greta Stoddart for her wise overview and detailed comments.

Much appreciation to Anne Pirie for the painting on the front cover, which suits the book so well. And of course thanks to Alwyn Marriage for her work as editor and publisher.

Finally I must also thank my cat, Koala, for his companionship in these isolating times and his great help in walking over the keyboard at crucial moments.

Contents

Self-portrait as a box of cards

Patience is written on me. I carry its history,
the flick and shuffle of fingers filling time.

My slivers of personality are stacked in two halves,
the gap between them thick enough to hold a ring.
                         I adore variety –
shape, colour, number, allegiance.
                         Give me an ace,
I'll find its scattered family. Order is what I love.

Of all my selves the joker is most used,
wrinkled with effort, a miniature on a stick
who doesn't understand complexity.

Boxed in I am safe, my corners shielded, hinged lid
splayed with much opening. I am old
but have survived well. You know what
to expect from me.
                My game is always my game.

Lewis chess queen

You sit contemplative, eyes downturned
as though life has always oppressed you.
Within your sad face a smile hovers.

I pick you up, feel your pitted surface,
your thickness and your delicacy.
I remember the warm fingers
that eased you from your rubber skin
then turned you over, the trial piece,
to see whether the rest of them
would come out better than you.

Bone recreated in plastic and black dye,
you have outlived the hands that shaped you.

Matchstick

Your dark headpiece
is ready to immolate itself for me.

Why were you created to burn yourself out?
Why don't you refuse?

Think of the tree you were part of.
Won't you miss the other fragments stolen from it?

You are wood; you don't need to be flame.
Hide yourself in the box, bury your head.

Don't go so meekly into incandescence;
save yourself before it's too late.

Leaving Cricklewood

Twenty-four years I've been here,
always about to move into wider space,
nestled in my cosy compromise,
with trains at the bottom of the garden
and rooms that are just that bit too small,
behind the Broadway that's never up-and-come.

You live in Cricklewood? Oh, how awful!
A joke place a step away from Neasden,
its roof dragons always poised to fly off
to somewhere that will have more dignity
than the fancy heart-shaped tombstones
awaiting their owners in Nodes's window.

Gone now are Green's Kosher Delicatessen
run by the Patels, the Barracuda Fish Bar
with its cloud of grease. Gone too
the daughter-in-law of the Armenian poet,
her wrinkled peppers and Cypriot beans,
and grinning *Me Amigo*'s Afro Wigs.

Now there's Mongolian Blue Sky, bread
spread with Polish lard, neither likely to stay,
ignored by the traffic that's always about
to end up somewhere else. I come back
to my flat that no one wants to buy,
that's still – for the moment – home.

My House

after Denise Levertov

She's someone who keeps her eyes open.
Sometimes she forgets to shade them
but she guards her modesty.

She welcomes you in but lets you know
the way to her heart is narrow
and not easy to find.

She likes to dress tastefully
but maybe overdoes the jewellery.
She doesn't shy away from colour.

Her grooming leaves much to be desired
but you can't help admiring her *chutzpah*
in showing herself as she is.

She's someone you could settle down and talk to,
a good sort, a shoulder to cry on,
an ample bosom, a strong pair of arms.

Curtained

This blue isn't cold. It's old and rich, deep as the far reaches of your unknown self. Its stripes have sheen, lights and darks blending into a near-night that strokes your spine. Too dark for sky, for most flowers, it's distilled down to its essence. When sky recedes behind street-lamps, blue covers the world outside, opens resonant spaces in white walls, hangs pleated and luxurious over the plants that rest against its pale lining. The colour warms me, chimes in a chord with vases, china, cushions that are smaller versions of itself. I fall through velvet into quiet.

Woodlice

Each frilled oval
is armour plating
a scrabble of legs
a front marked
by hair-fine feelers.

Sometimes I find
lone ones or pairs
skimming the floor
or crisped in corners.
They make me wonder

what hidden slime
has lured them here
what unknown rot
seeps through the house
feeding them decay.

Intruders

They've slid from earth to concrete,
squashing under doors, glutted

with yesterday's rain-fresh feast
of pulmonaria and chard.

Last night, a wet kiss on my bare foot,
a flattened oval stuck fast to the floor,

a loaf-brown turd lying in a track
of slime across the breadboard.

In the morning, crazed silver trails
on carpets, doormats, worktops.

They slip off early. One lies
curved and flaccid in a mucous pool;

the rest gather their strength
for tomorrow night.

Darker than Green

At first only a speck
that spreads while you're not looking,
it creeps into corners,
settles, colonises,
breeds
in crevices you didn't know were there.

Insidious is the word.
It soils, contaminates,
leaves nothing pure.
You can tell at once
it's rotten.

Soon you've forgotten
what it's like to enjoy
a clean room,
your own life.

Predator

It must be dead already,
the slack body in the bath,
legs stiff, toes outstretched,
feet reaching out for
the bathmat's rough pile.

Later I find smears
the same red as the mat,
a glistening raw wound,
a squashed grey mess
extruded from damp fur.

Nowhere to be seen –
the killer's wide-eyed face,
the gleam of his sharp teeth,
his unabashed pursuit
of his own pleasure.

Caught

a lipogram

You can't run away. Nobody can go out of doors or pull curtains
back from shut windows. Walls block all roads, guards turn
lay-bys into instant prisons.

What can you do, in your tiny caravan? Wait for faded day,
for moon-shadow. Don't wait too long. Soon you must think
of crawling out into dark, facing what you most shrink from:
rats scuttling, arachnid limbs, sounds of pain from dark
yards. You would flinch from iron-shod kicks, a stinging lash.

Go now. Night falls, its black prongs gashing ground. Go out.
Push that last boundary.

Not your fault

You couldn't stop your dog
shitting on the doorstep. The stone
flew through the window by accident.

You must have dropped your lighter.
A pity the spark should have happened
to catch the Polish house.

It was nothing to do with you.
How could you possibly have known
they were inside? You'd gone home

before the smoke-shocked faces,
the arms stripped to glistening flesh,
the child they kept trying to wake.

Kristallnacht

It happened a long time ago. They showed it on television
in shades of grey. It started with smashed windows, the
glass jagged over black space inside. *Jude* was smeared
in ugly writing on some of the windows. Men in uniform
were marching down the street, young men with short,
short haircuts and bland faces looking straight forward.
Then people were running to get away. Some of them
seemed pleased, but then there were others with stars pinned
to their clothes who looked frightened as the fires came near.
In the film old people spoke who had been children then.
At the time they didn't understand what was happening;
later they understood. A man opened a box and took out
the yellow star he'd kept for seventy years.

Pink

You never liked pink –
roses and marshmallows
and bows for girls' hair.

You always liked yellow –
sun and lemons
and the number seven.

If you'd lived back then
you might have been given
a pink triangle and a yellow star.

Industrial process

First they are assembled
packed tight like components
not made to come apart
thoroughly stripped
of everything extraneous.

The technology is simple:
a few pipes, a stopcock
a door with a good seal
operatives to make sure
they all fit inside.

It doesn't take long:
the agent does its job
with maximum efficiency.
After a waiting period
the waste is cleared away.

Homeland

Before you came, what we knew were olive trees,
mules scuffling through dust, sweet smoke
of cooking and tobacco, old women polishing
stories generations long. The church bell clanged
the regularity of our life; the language of our land
had not been wrested from us.

You were the refugees, returning to the home
you mourned each year with brine and bitter herbs,
digging through stones, watering your new life
as it grew into our soil. At the beginning it seemed
we could have lived together. Semite was not a word
you applied only to yourselves.

Our home became your right. We gagged on smoke
from burning fields, watched our olives fall
ungathered from the trees as our compliant mules
bore us away from houses you had stolen.
Church bells hung mute; the language we heard
was like ours but not ours. Old women's stories
were uprooted from the land.

Now we are the strangers. Caged inside
our villages of ash and rubble, our children
do not understand what the future means.
We grow as weeds in your God-given soil;
only hate feeds us in the harsh desert light.
The meat of our life has been ripped from its bones.
You have taken from us the right to care.

To the Wire

from a photograph by Mei Lim

Be thankful for wire mesh
for through it you can see blue,
can tell if the grass on the other side
really would be greener.

Be thankful for its top
for over it you can see clouds,
can know the sky is yours
and has not been bought.

Be thankful for its holes
for through them you can feel air,
can smell the way people live
in the other country.

Be thankful for its edge
for under it you could crawl out
of your imprisoning day
into a different life.

Laudemus

Let us praise the sky, the extravagant blue of it,
the air that lets us breathe joy.
Let us praise the ground that stops us being unhinged
                                   from the earth,
our feet that carry us and hold us there,
the shoes that keep our feet from getting hurt.

Let us praise little things, the use we make of them,
keys that give us entry to our lives, paper clips
that keep our thoughts together, cups that make tea possible.
Let us praise light switches, gas taps, radiator keys,
plugs that connect us to a comfortable life.

Let us praise the earth and all its species,
bank voles who scuffle under leaves, pangolins
like walking pine cones, sea otters who sleep holding hands,
the kilotonnes of krill that blue whales swallow.
Let us praise purple loosestrife that shades our ponds.

Let us praise people, the billions who breathe the air
and love the sky and tread the ground and are alive,
Let us praise all life, that keeps on living itself.

Gardener

He liked to caress the names of plants –
penstemon, hemerocallis, euphorbia, cerinthe –
eyed every leaf, fondled them into growth
watched colour erupt from sepals, buds open
on the swagger of stamens. Each flowering
was a tiny consummation. He liked too
tearing out weeds, taking revenge on those
that dared eclipse his darlings. In other beds
ripe fruit tempted him to excess, the crush
of raspberries on the palate, the downy cheeks
of apricot or peach. At night he dreamt
fecundity, next day would mulch and cosset
to bring on more. He followed his passion alone;
no human life had shared it since the spring
when one neglected seedling had failed to thrive.

Water Lily

Dropped in, rooted in her pot,
she's more mysterious
than seed planted in soil.
Her leaves, sunk deep below sunlight,
may never re-emerge.

I hope for heart-shaped platters
sustaining waxy cups,
their toothed edges protecting
a ring of tasselled gold.
I believe in the jewel inside.

I stare down through thick water,
see nothing of her at all.
After a while, impatient,
I fish her up again, to find
an embryonic leaf,
a newt scrabbling in mud.

Colonised

I dig up a dandelion. The root breaks. These roots are long;
they reach deep into the soil. I throw the plant on the compost
heap with its damaged companions. The rest lie quiet and
wilted; this stump flails about, seeking earth. The dandelions
in the flower beds crane their stems towards me, flare bright
with indignation. Globes of downy seeds, light and innocent,
explode towards me; I'm showered with tiny parachutes. My
skin itches where they land, an itch that burrows beyond the
skin. I sense rootlets, subtle and insistent as ingrown hairs.
Soon jagged green leaves cover me so closely they weave into
a coat. Their tap roots knit together in my muscles, preparing
to bore through bone.

Mouldiwarp

snout go first   snouting earth smell
smell worm
                              squish of eat
push on   push earth
hard earth want water
more water
                              more wormsquish
                              more push

                              find way through
shove shovelling forward
big claws shove
body push
                              snout jangle
                                        on stonehard

                              body stop
                                        hurt

scrabblefeetscrabblefeet

                                        clawdig
push shove
                              snout feel worm
moreworm

hard   snout janglehurt
janglehurtjanglehurt

                              heavy stomp
                                        earth fall in

Snails

When you stop to look
no two shells are the same:
meticulous spirals
layered, striated, pinwheeled,
each one a world
travelling with viscous grace
on its soft-bodied carrier.

When you don't stop
you hear the crunch.
Oozing, grey,
harder than eggshell underfoot,
a smashed life you could have saved.
You excuse murder, tell yourself
they would have eaten your plants.

Rarely you may see them
making love, soft body stuck
to soft body, slime more naked
than human skin, feelers
caressing one another,
eyes looking out
from supple watchtowers.

Sparrow Fall

Are not two sparrows sold for a farthing? and one of them
shall not fall on the ground without your Father.

Matthew 10:29

These birds weren't 'nature'.
We knew them in the garden
before school taught them to us,
their soft intricacy of London browns –
earth and wood and pavement dust –

the way their heads cocked on one side
to look at us, how they'd eat
breadcrumbs from grass. *Only sparrows,*
we'd say, preferring brighter visitors:
starlings, blue tits, a rare jay.

Now we search for them in the morning,
have to be satisfied with blackbirds.
We wonder where they've got to, why
London has almost abolished them,
why their lives were worth so little.

Switchew Birds

Itch-itch-itch-itchyswitchew
Itch-itch-itch-itchyswitchew

The birds' voices, like a sneeze,
sing morning light from a window
too high for me to see.

Outside the bedroom walls,
cream paint blistered with damp,
the uncut grass is bent with dew

hiding the huge step down
to the steep lawn
where I'm not allowed to go.

The birds' song is grass,
the rush of feet meeting green
the spicy yellow smell of its decay.

The switchew birds
are speaking to me
their unknown language
naming everything.

Therapy Session

And my husband said ...
I listen, reel in
the tangled wires,
nod, look up

and see across the road
the graceful flap
of a heron landing
on a bungalow roof.

It stands, orders itself
like a shaken umbrella,
stretches its neck,
flies off. I nod.

Give me a phrase with white wings

thoughtless
steered by stars
whose skies it occupies.

I want a cyclical dependable word
out at elbows or tense-thighed.
I lack the balance otherwise.

I am a maker of songs.
I make vowels from objects.
Don't give me an hysterical word
or I shall weep.

Phrases taken from Migrant *by Vahni Capildeo*

Honey

Some afternoons bees alight on the page,
bodies linked in a poem
that runs, moves, settles in no shape
till it is caught in honey.

Other days the sealed honeycomb
waits for the blade to prise its sweetness,
the larvae retired into cells where,
not yet flown free of the paper,
a poem sleeps.

Poet

For a few weeks I thought I was a poet. Someone said to me,
You're a poet, and my imagination grew several feet taller.
My hair became branches that sported blossom; one of my
fingernails sharpened into a pen that ran painlessly with ink
whenever it touched paper. Words poured from my pores;
I only had to scoop them from the floor and they would shape
themselves into stanzas. Rhyme chimed in my voice and my
body moved in metre. Poetry and I were so closely related
you could hardly tell us apart.

Then the poems told me they needed to be read. I gathered
them up and sent them to a place where I hoped they'd find a
home. Soon they started meeting other poems. Those poems
didn't just grow blossom: they landscaped whole gardens and
garnered stars by the handful. My words felt drab. They
clutched their coats around them and huddled in a corner.

Before long my branches were bare. My fingernail broke and
ran red with blood. The dust I swept from the floor could
barely make a line of prose and the stanzas were empty
rooms. My imagination shrank, and each blank sheet
stripped me of the title Poet. Then one day words arrived,
made their bow and started writing themselves.

A fin in a waste of waters

Virginia Woolf on beginning to write The Waves

look
a whole book
empty for you to write your thoughts in
what a dare   a shark's fin
slicing through crinkled water that

laps
and then slaps
against you   you keep diving to find
those places in your mind
where your words might surface again

wait
not too late
to dive once more for the hoard you missed
the long-ago drowned kist
where memories have been growing

pull
a handful
from its inside   gently guide them up
soon they will flower   cup
each one in your hand   let them speak

know
how their slow
unfolding brings you closer to words
to voices not yet heard
take your pen   go after the fin

The husband

From the start some things puzzled him:
the strange shadow that played around her legs
her plaits' gleam like angel hair at low tide
the way she was only happy when in the bath
how she'd eat nothing but raw fish and seaweed
though she wasn't Japanese; her great love
of sitting on rocks, gazing beyond the waves.

He never could remember how they'd met
had no idea what kept her close to him
when she spoke so little and her words
rose like bubbles from deep inside her body
in a language he only half understood.
He noticed how her kisses tasted of salt
felt her slither away when they made love.

While she was with him he learned to forget time.
Each night their room became a watery cave
quicksilvered with shoals of fish; the furniture
turned to corals that pulsed and swayed. Her eyes
changed from blue to green to grey as the light
came and went before them, while he swam
in this new element, following after her.

Each morning he awoke in their dry bed
with her beside him writhing in discontent
till it was time for her to take her bath.
One day he reached out, touched empty space,
kissed the pillow which tasted of her salt.
He went down to the shore. She'd left her clothes
in the shape of the shadow, shoes splayed like fins.

Music

At the beginning there was only blue,
water's dense weight as I cut through it,
the power of muscle and tail.

Then came sound pushing through water,
its dance on my skin a bright shiver
down the length of my spine.

I don't know when sound became song,
a voice and body, another shape
sensed without seeing

only that near me water thickened
and warmed. My hesitant voice
called in answer to yours.

I never think dark will come

all I am is pulse and heave
waves altered each moment by light

day is slow to warm me

I know the sun's wide road
only when my surface tingles
with glitter points that flash and spark

deep down I am always dark

clouds shade me through green and beyond
their arrows of rain darken me before night
so I lose the sun without finding the moon

the fade of day covers me with grey gauze
and I bask in the sweet fire that lingers over me

sometimes light slopes away in secret
stealing my warmth   blinding me to myself
till all I know is my own movement

I never think light will return

Fallen Night

Clouds hover, long bars like pink candy in water-blue sky, till dark covers them. The sun has dropped behind the hills; the birds are silenced. The end of a numberless series of days, each with its own ending. The end of light. No glint of grass blades, no orange flare of nasturtiums, no scatter of sparks from cold granite. The moon has lost its way. No trace of it in the extinguished sky, no possibility of calling it back from the night before when, thin as a nail-paring, it hung suspended in black that was blue. No stars. Everywhere they are ending, leaving gaps in the universe. Everywhere we are ending; each night souls flicker out. A day has died; we must not forget to mourn. After death, unthinkable for now, comes birth.

Description

I don't often trouble now
to describe cornfields

the way the corn stands upright
waiting for execution
the way the harvester
strikes it down in regiments

the way mice and birds
are sacrificed to our hunger
leaving only the crows
to scavenge through the stubble.

Does it still bother me,
all this killing: that death
flushes us out
from between the stalks?

I don't often trouble now
to describe myself:
how it no longer matters
who I am.

The lines in italics come from one of Virginia Woolf's last diary entries.

Body

We don't know how long it will be
before you and I have to divorce.
I hope it will be amicable and our parting
won't cause us too much pain. I know for you
it will be the end. I'll be sorry to leave you.

We've been together a long time, so close
we could be one and the same. I can't say
our relationship is an easy one. Often
I don't treat you as well as you deserve;
sometimes you hurt me or let me down.
I don't always like you the way you are;
you keep telling me there's only so much
you can change.

I hope we won't be splitting up just yet.
We're a good couple.

Obituary

She spent many of her years
looking for herself, only to find
wide open space. She learned to love
when it was almost too late,
wrote less than she could have,
was an expert at wasting time.

She cared passionately for some
of the wrong things, overlooked
too many of the right ones. She tried
not to harm but did less good
than she would have wished.

She enjoyed gardens, jokes,
quirks other people didn't notice,
the company of old friends.
She didn't much like big cities
or loud music or people who intruded.

She read like a scavenger, loved songs
that made her cry, sought out
what some might call God.
She didn't want to die but learned
to school herself for death.

Professional

Outside, people are walking, their life
not yet extinguished. In here
the dead lie in muted dark.

There's no conversation, only cold.
Inside its casket, a vacated body
seems as if it stirs.

I remember my father
after his last breath,
the faint shudder I thought I saw.

The bell rings. I leave quiet bodies
to meet the living laid bare by loss.
I wish I could stop their crying,

say to them, Look, the dead
are at peace now. *How can I help?*
– Just bring him back to life.

Jay's Grave

I've tried to sleep for more than a hundred years
in this grass triangle, juddered by cars,
prodded by sheep feet, explained by walkers
who know me only as a landmark on a map.

My softened bones are sunk into dark peat
juicy with streams and urine and trapped rain.
My flesh melts through the mulch of leaves;
atoms of my blood infuse the heather.

Once I brought lilies in tall vases to rooms filled
with others' pleasure. Now people bring me
buttercups, campion, rosebay willow-herb,
flowers I wouldn't have given a second look.

This apron-shaped bed won't let me forget
the service I bore, doing always for them
what no one did for me. He made me
the silent vessel for all his consequences.

They denied me my rest where others lie
secure in their righteousness. They left me here,
tilted hills behind me and a bracken field,
alone with the wide moor and the cradling sky.

*According to Dartmoor legend, the roadside grave near Natsworthy is that
of a young woman, Kitty Jay, who became pregnant and committed suicide.*

Clouds

They're layered over the moor
like ruched cotton wool,
twisted, folded, pleated,
a darker stripe
on top of a long fillet
drawn out into a thin strand.

Suspended above the hills
as if on strings
they're overlaid
on a blue backdrop,
ranged one behind the other
like scenery flats.
Near the horizon they're dense,
edges blobbed, smeared,
painted with a loose brush.

High up it's as as though
they've been pulled apart,
spread more thinly,
diluted like thick cream
in water that isn't water,
translucent colour
that isn't really there.

Savouring the moor

The sky tastes wet with a tinge of frost;
clouds are denser and hint at sugar.
You can munch grassy hills, crunch
the salted brown of bracken, slurp
yellow gorse till it sings on the palate,
savour each tiny difference of green,
balance bitter and sweet and salt.
Lichens are like nothing else, a faint
aftertaste of fresh, or a piquant zing
you can't hold in your mouth.

Wearing shoes makes your feet stupid

Ajahn Chah, Thai Buddhist teacher

Released from cosseting
foot becomes pensive,
contemplates the ache
of cold grass on heel
and softened skin, nostalgic,
as wet seeps between toes,
for sand, the play of tide,
sole's soft dream in mud.
Each lift and bend
brings your foot more alive;
your toes quiver
with their new intelligence.

Rite

I stand in my white gown straight as a candle,
my mirrored face wondering at what I have been.

My hands lift the crown plaited from nightshade,
red stems of dogwood, rosemary, jasmine.

It catches my hair as it finds its right place.
I step outside into soft warm day.

It holds my head close as I thread down the bank,
legs stung by nettles, feet stabbed by stones.

The water smells sweet, of light and summer.
My toes squeeze mud, slide to the rim where

heat meets with cold, new edges of water
tickle old land. Here I take breath,

grateful for air, stride through the cling
of long heavy white, plunge with closed eyes —

lose all that I was. I climb out of myself
on the far bank, uncrowned and whole.

Awakening

Life sits in my hands
an object I've forgotten the use of,
a quill pen, a nutmeg grater
or a toy played with once —

a wooden fire-engine
whose people, coloured differently
all with the same face
fit peg-like in their round slots.

What did I see in that? I ask
What is it for? turning it over
wishing I could ignore
the feel of it in my fingers

could grasp why ink
or nutmeg or the wooden people
should have mattered so much.
Then once again I know.

Paradise

Late afternoon smells of earth,
damp grass, far-off smoke.
Light softens to mist. Rooks
crrk unseen in fading trees.

Walking slows,
each step a discovery,
each breath the only one
I've ever known.

Grass blades weave
a basket of shadows.
In their green deception
these might-be tomatoes

rise from the ground on stalks:
five waxy globes
half-open, like parachutes
descended to earth.

The Croatian/Serbian word for tomato is paradajz – paradise

Angel

The other day an angel
wrapped soft grey wings around me,
feather-tips touching my heart.

I hadn't expected it to visit. It said
it had come to stay, and smiled
the way I hoped an angel would smile.

I leaned back against it, cushioned
from the shock of being human.
My naked skin felt its own feathers.
I remembered I could fly.

To Pray

You never know when it's going to find you
that moment when sight becomes prayer
nor can you say it will happen
when the sun wakes green hills
or the apple tree's clenched pink buds
release their guarded selves
or the river glimpsed through trees
becomes light liquefied.

Sometimes you don't know it as beauty
that moment when song or birdcall
trickles deep through your silence
or the sound of cars or a distant mower
is so much itself you want to worship it
when a sign in a London street
fills you so full of colour
you can only stand and breathe it.

Benediction

That afternoon the hills were in a huff.
Grass was exhausted, far less than green.
Sky sulked behind a tattered veil of wool,
flat scraps of leaves clumped in a dowdy mess.

The day was thrown away, already lost
dropping useless as a fallen twig.
I turned my back and left it to its ruin,
my feet insulted by the encroach of mud.

Across the field sheep leapt in surprise;
one stared, gentle in the lowering light.
Then, on the way home, I saw.
                              In front of hills
green as themselves once more, caressed by sky,
four rose-hips dangled from a pergola,
deep red, each one a sacrament.

Coming home

to the rise of breath
the dark space behind thought
the feel of feet on ground